This book is so fun! Have 'in this book! Do you like it? I think it is really fun because it is full of activetys. Fill this book with words.

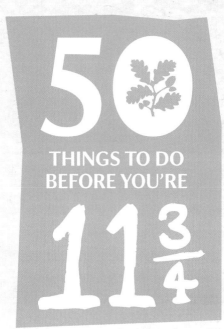

50

THINGS TO DO BEFORE YOU'RE

11 ¾

50

THINGS TO DO
BEFORE YOU'RE

11 $\frac{3}{4}$

My EXTRA MESSY Adventure Notebook

National Trust

Written by
Nicole Daw and Hannah Jones McVey

First published in the United Kingdom in 2015 by
National Trust Books
1 Gower Street, London WC1E 6HD

An imprint of Pavilion Books Group Ltd

© National Trust 2015
The National Trust is a registered charity, no. 205846

Designed for the National Trust by 18 feet and rising. Based on
original concept and content by Behaviour Change with design work
by N. Duncan Mills.

Photographs: © National Trust Images/Naomi Goggin 6; © National Trust
Images/Paul Harris 13, 26, 74, 94; © National Trust Images/David Levenson 7,
9, 11; © National Trust Images/John Millar 2, 14; © National Trust Images/John
Miller 83; © National Trust Images/Chris O'Reilly 74; © National Trust Images/
Ian Shaw 5, 50; © National Trust Images/Megan Taylor 38.

© Alamy/ DonSmith 77; © Alamy/ funkyfood London – Paul Williams 82;
© Alamy/ Tim Gainey 78; © Alamy/ Maskot 76; © Alamy/ Selecta 85;
© Alamy/ Jill Stephenson 76; © Alamy/ Tony Tallec 84.

Illustrations by Richard Horne

ISBN: 978-1-909881-41-9

A CIP catalogue record for this book is available from the British Library.

10 9 8 7 6 5 4 3 2

Reproduction by Mission Productions Ltd, Hong Kong
Printed by 1010 Printing International Ltd, China

This book can be ordered direct from the publisher at
the website www.pavilionbooks.com, or try your local
bookshop. Also available at National Trust shops and
nationaltrustbooks.co.uk

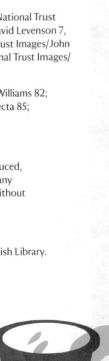

CONTENTS

50 messy things to do before you're 11¾   8
Getting ready ✓   10
How to clean up ✓   12

FILTHY

1. Create compost trousers   16
2. Slip down a mud slide ✓   17
3. Make a fat ball bird feeder   18
4. Walk barefoot on a mud safari   19
5. Play a twisty messy game ✓   20
6. Mountain bike through mud   21
7. Build a troll's cave   22
8. Go barefoot painting ✓   23
9. Help build a cob wall   24
10. Design a pair of messy memory trousers   25

STICKY

11. Invent an egg protector   28
12. Make toffee apples ✓   29
13. Create with clay ✓   30
14. Build a giant nest   31
15. Target practice with mud and a spoon ✓   32
16. Make damper bread over a fire   33
17. Create a masterpiece with natural paints ✓   34
18. Throw seed bombs ✓   35
19. Dream up a miniature world ✓   36
20. Carve a pumpkin lantern ✓   37

MUCKY

21. Leave monster tracks ✓ 40
22. Become a worm charmer 41
23. Build a conker run ✓ 42
24. Help out on a farm ✓ 43
25. Brew a stinky magic potion 44
26. Dry your own mud bricks 45
27. Make feely boxes 46
28. Dissect an owl pellet 47
29. Set up a mud kitchen 48
30. Grow seedy socks 49

GRUBBY

31. Give a tree a face ✓ 52
32. Make an earth angel ✓ 53
33. Disappear into the
    landscape ✓ 54
34. Make a charcoal pencil 55
35. Build a sand sea monster ✓56
36. Create a wild
    assault course 57
37. Make patterns with sand 58
38. Build a wormery 59
39. Make chalk prints ✓ 60
40. Build a scarecrow ✓ 61

SOGGY

41. Become a welly engineer 64
42. Paint with water 65
43. Go on a puddle hunt ✓ 66
44. Give a toad a home 67
45. Have a water relay ✓ 68
46. Go on a seaweed safari 69
47. Bridge a puddle 70
48. Make your own
    bubble wand 71
49. Go on a wet welly walk 72
50. Set out a snail picnic 73

10 best things to do 74

The best things to do
throughout the year 86

50 messy things to do before you're 11¾

Welcome to the great outdoors, this time with a pinch of extra mess to get stuck into... Roll your sleeves up, put your wellies on and start splashing in those muddy puddles. Whether you're at the park, in the woods or on a beach, there are plenty of ideas for endless fun. You'll find grubby experiments, filthy games, soggy fun and a lot of sticky messes for all you mucky pups out there.

We've put together a list of the greatest 50 messy challenges for you to complete before you reach 11¾, and we're making it as easy as pie – mud pie, of course – to do them somewhere near you.

The only question is, are you messy enough to complete all 50?

Note to grown-ups: Children matter to the National Trust, so we recommend that all these activities are supervised by an adult – at a distance. We trust that you will make your own judgement about what is safe and suitable for the ability of your child. Just remember to stand back, keep smiling and get stuck in if you dare!

Caution: Some of them may cause extreme dirtiness (and you might have to have your hair washed).

9

GETTING READY

Preparation is the key to extra fun messy adventures. Take a camera to record your achievements and take this book with you, too. You never know, you might be able to tick a few off the list each time you go out and we promise that we don't mind if you get this book mucky.

Take wet wipes and hand gel just in case you get some extra yukky messy gloop on you.

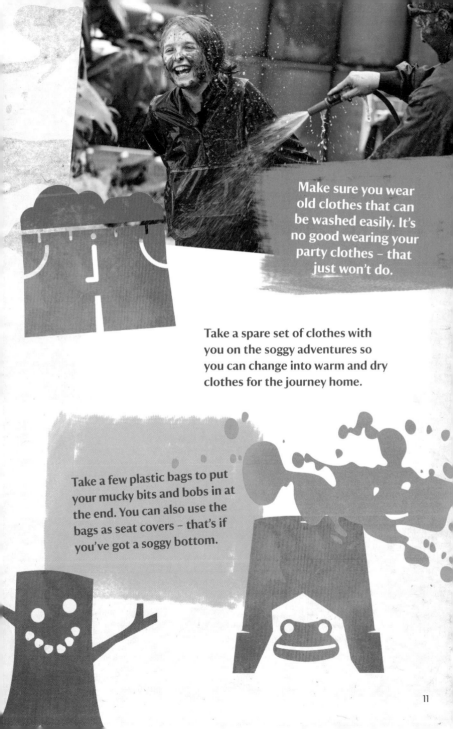

Make sure you wear old clothes that can be washed easily. It's no good wearing your party clothes – that just won't do.

Take a spare set of clothes with you on the soggy adventures so you can change into warm and dry clothes for the journey home.

Take a few plastic bags to put your mucky bits and bobs in at the end. You can also use the bags as seat covers – that's if you've got a soggy bottom.

HOW TO CLEAN UP

It's always fun getting messy, but not so much fun cleaning up afterwards. Why not try to do the really messy challenges on days when you need a bath anyway – you know you're going to have to wash your hair on a Sunday night, so make it extra messy just in time! You can enjoy watching the bath water turn a muddy brown colour – job done.

Make sure you wash your hands at the end of each adventure with warm soap and water. Dry them properly, too.

If your wellies are especially muddy, try to find a clean-ish puddle to walk through on the way home. This should remove most of the mud. You can also find a clump of grass to wipe your wellies on.

Last but not least: remember to take your wellies off BEFORE you go into the house (otherwise you'll get us into trouble)!

13

FILTHY

 1.   Create compost trousers

 2.   Slip down a mud slide ✓

 3.   Make a fat ball bird feeder

 4.   Walk barefoot on a
mud safari

 5.   Play a twisty messy game ✓

 6.   Mountain bike through mud

 7.   Build a troll's cave

 8.   Go barefoot painting ✓

 9.   Help build a cob wall

 10. Design a pair of messy
memory trousers

1. CREATE COMPOST TROUSERS

A messy task with amazing results

What you need:

- An old pair of trousers, the bigger the better
- String
- Vegetable peel and scraps
- Shredded newspaper or dry leaves
- Strong sticky tape

> **TOP TIP**
>
> It will help your compost along if you mix it occasionally. The little space at the top of the trousers means you can give them a good shake without opening them up.

Take a pair of trousers and tie the end of the legs with string. Stuff a layer as deep as your hand of vegetable peelings, tea bags and old flowers into each leg. Then stuff a finger's-depth of shredded newspaper or dry leaves on top. Repeat this until the legs are full. Roll the top of the trousers down, leaving a little space at the top and tape them shut with tape. Leave in a dry corner for three months, then undo the string and shake the compost out of the legs on to your flowerbeds or veggie patch.

What did you use in your compost?

Date completed: Day _____ Month _____ Year _____

2. SLIP DOWN A MUD SLIDE

Slidey fun is guaranteed!

What you need:

- Water
- Dirt

Find a good slope for your slide. The best one won't have any roots or bits sticking up which may hurt you on the way down. A grass slope will turn to mud but it will take time. A mud slope gets better and better the more times you slide down, so pour some water down and get sliding.

TOP TIP

If the slope won't go muddy use a tarpaulin (waterproof sheet) attached to the ground with tent pegs and mix up soil and water in a bucket to make your mud. Throw it down your slide and off you go!

Smear some of the mud here and draw yourself sliding down it.

Date completed: Day _25TH_ Month _August_ Year _2015_

3. MAKE A FAT BALL BIRD FEEDER

Attract birds to your garden with this delicious but messy snack

What you need:

- A lump of lard
- Bird seed
- String
- Pine cone
- A bowl for mixing
- Warm water for hand washing

Birds need food all year round but especially in the winter when their natural foods are scarce and in the spring when they are feeding their young. In your bowl mix your dollop of lard with the bird seed mix until the seeds are evenly spread and the lard is soft. Then cover the pine cone with your mixture to form a ball.

Once your fat ball is in place it might take the birds a few days to find it. Watch quietly from a distance. What types of bird visit your fat ball? Write a list here:

Date completed: Day _____ Month _____ Year _____

4. WALK BAREFOOT ON A MUD SAFARI

Feel the mud squelch between your toes on this mucky adventure

What you need:

- Mud

There are great muddy places in woodlands, near ponds and along farm tracks. Make sure you know what is underneath and around you and avoid deep water. When you have located a good patch of mud throw off your shoes and socks and get squelching!

TOP TIP

If you are enjoying your barefoot safari why not take it further and see what the forest floor, wet grass, gravel and moss feel like.

Stamp a muddy footprint on this page:

Why not try number 8 and go barefoot painting with those muddy feet?

Date completed: Day _____ Month _____ Year _____

I

5. PLAY A TWISTY MESSY GAME

Left hand mud, right hand leaves...

What you need:

– At least one person to play with

Pick four different natural materials such as leaves, mud, moss and dust. Build up six piles of each material in four rows next to each other. Take turns challenging each other to place one hand on one pile and a foot on another.

TOP TIP

Make two dice out of little square boxes. On one write 'left leg', 'right leg', 'left hand', 'right hand' on four sides and 'choose your own' on the last two. On the other, write your four materials on four sides and 'choose your own' on the last two. Throw these dice to decide where you will have to go next.

I did all of them

Write down what you used in each pile:

water

mud

leafs

paint

Date completed: Day **6TH** Month **December** Year **2016**

20

6. MOUNTAIN BIKE THROUGH MUD

Slip and slide your way around a track

What you need:

- A mountain bike
- A cycling helmet

Go after or during rain when tracks are really muddy. Ride straight through the puddles and try and balance through the muddy patches. See if you can build up your confidence, starting with smaller challenges and building up from there.

TOP TIP

Wear goggles to stop mud splashing in your eyes. You can just wipe them clean and keep on going.

Gently press this page onto your bike tyre to create a muddy imprint.

Some National Trust properties have special bike trails for you to follow. Check online for your nearest one at nationaltrust.org.uk/visit/activities/cycling/

Date completed: Day __17__ Month __February__ Year __2016__

7. BUILD A TROLL'S CAVE

Use mud, dirt and rotting wood to create a horrid home fit for a troll

What you need:

- The world around you
- A guide to troll architecture (See below)

Trolls love muddy floors, smelly corners and damp walls. Find a dark space like a fallen tree or a pile of rocks to create the back of the cave. Use mud bricks (see number 26 to see how) to build a doorway and then create the other walls and roof with mud, pond weed, dirt and anything else you think a grimy troll might like.

TOP TIP

If you have ruined a pair of socks during your messy adventures, cut them up and use them to make the perfect troll carpet.

Take a photo of your troll cave and stick it here:

Date completed: Day _____ Month _____ Year _____

26ᵀᴴ January 2015

8. GO BAREFOOT PAINTING
Shoes off, socks off, paint on!

What you need:
- √ – Paper
- √ – Paint
- √ – Water to wash your feet

Run around on a piece of paper with paint-covered feet to make a crazy pattern. Slip or tiptoe across to change the shapes that you make or decorate the footprints to create a clever picture.

TOP TIP

Print your feet next to each other. When you step away you will see the print left looks a little like butterfly wings. Let them dry, then add a body and a head.

What did it feel like to have paint on your feet?

strange

Date completed: Day __26ᵀᴴ__ Month __January__ Year __2015__

23

9. HELP BUILD A COB WALL

Get mucky with straw and mud

What you need:

- Soil
- Finely cut straw
- Water

TOP TIP

You can mould cob into any shape you want. You could also draw patterns or write your name on the surface.

Cob is a building material made with earth, straw and water that has been used since the prehistoric times to build houses and walls. Lots of old houses in Britain were built using cob. Add water to the soil to make a sticky mess then mix in some straw to make it stronger. Use your bare feet and hands to mix it together. When your cob is ready, build up a thick layer then wait for it to dry. You can then build another layer on top and repeat this process again and again until your wall is complete.

Take a photo of you and your completed cob wall and stick it on this page.

Date completed: Day _____ Month _____ Year _____

10. DESIGN A PAIR OF MESSY MEMORY TROUSERS

Get the most from your messy clothes

What you need:

- An old pair of trousers
- Paint

If your mess up a pair of trousers so much that you can't use them any more why not turn them into the ultimate messy trousers! Paint them in camouflage colours or with pictures of your favourite messy activities. Once they are dry you can use them next time you head out on a messy adventure.

Draw a picture of your memory trousers here:

Date completed: Day _____ Month _____ Year _____

STICKY

 11. Invent an egg protector

 12. Make toffee apples

 13. Create with clay √

 14. Build a giant nest

 15. Target practice with mud and a spoon

 16. Make damper bread over a fire

 17. Create a masterpiece with √ natural paints

 18. Throw seed bombs √

 19. Dream up a miniature world √

 20. Carve a pumpkin lantern √

11. INVENT AN EGG PROTECTOR

Will your egg survive?

What you need:

- An egg (not cooked!)
- String
- Sticky tape
- Moss, sticks and other natural materials

TOP TIP

If you squeeze an egg in your hand, making sure the pressure is even all the way round, it won't break. Are you brave enough to try?

Your challenge: to wrap your egg in natural materials, throw it and see if it breaks. Moss might cushion the landing; mud might create a protective shell. When you are ready, throw your egg down a hill, out of a window, or as high as you can and let it drop to the floor. If you have a brave friend, you could try playing a game of catch with it! Open up your protection and see if the egg is still in one piece. If it isn't it can get very messy!

Draw a diagram of your protector here:

Fact: When an egg is in its nest a chicken will sit on it with the point facing upwards. This helps the egg not to crack.

Date completed: Day _____ Month _____ Year _____

12. MAKE TOFFEE APPLES

Apples picked straight from a tree taste wonderful. Have a go at turning them into sticky toffee apples.

What you need:

- Apples
- 4 wooden lolly sticks
- Stove or a fire pit with a grate
- Pan
- Wooden spoon
- Kitchen scales

- 200g golden caster sugar
- ½ teaspoon of vinegar
- 2 tablespoons of golden syrup
- 50ml of water
- Greaseproof paper
- A grown-up to help you

To make toffee you need a lot of heat, so make sure you have some help from a grown-up. First, place the apple on a firm surface and twist off the stalk. Push your lolly stick all the way into the apple from the top until it is secure. Tip the water and sugar into a pan over a medium heat and stir for 5 minutes until the sugar has dissolved. Add the vinegar and syrup. Bring it to the boil and keep stirring. You can check that it is ready by dripping a small drop into cold water. If it is ready the drip should be hard when you fish it out. Quickly dip your apples into the toffee and put them on a piece of greaseproof paper to harden.

How did your toffee apple taste? Write the best words you can think to describe it here:

sticky crunchy toffie apple

Date completed: Day _11TH_ Month _December_ Year _2016_

29

13. CREATE WITH CLAY

Find some clay on a river bank and get creative

What you need:
- ✓ Clay
- ✗ – Water
- ✗ – A shovel or a trowel

Clay is a kind of thick, sticky earth that is found all over the country and has been used to make things for thousands of years. River banks are an excellent place to find clay – ask an adult to help you – but you might even be able to find some in your garden by digging a hole. Take a lump of clay and use a tiny bit of water to work it into a ball. You can now make whatever you like with it – a pot, a model of your favourite animal or of a monster.

What colour was the clay you found? Smear a little bit here as a reminder:

grey

Date completed: Day __1st__ Month __December__ Year __2016__

14. BUILD A GIANT NEST

How big will yours be?

What you need:

- Moss, sticks and other natural materials
- Mud

The recipe for a great nest is very simple. Find lots of sticks, big ones and little ones, and arrange them in a circle on the floor. Start building the walls up using mud to stick the sticks together. If you are near a river you can use some clay for extra stickiness. Crisscross the sticks to make your nest stronger, and remember that small ones can be really good for filling gaps and holding everything together.

> **TOP TIP**
>
> Most birds line their nests with soft materials such as feathers, moss and grasses. Have a go at filling your nest with soft things and snuggle in.

Imagine a giant bird decides to live in your nest. Draw a picture of what it might look like.

> Some kinds of birds make nests out of their own spit. People take these nests and turn them into soup!

Date completed: Day _____ Month _____ Year _____

31

15. TARGET PRACTICE WITH MUD AND A SPOON

Mess is guaranteed in this target challenge

What you need:

- A Spoon
- Mud
- Chalk

Create a target by drawing a circle with chalk on a tree or a wall. Small circles will be a harder challenge to hit than big ones. Take your spoon and fill it up with mud. Hold the handle tightly between your thumb and first finger with the spoon pointing towards you. Use a finger on your other hand to press down on the top of the spoon before letting go and watch your mud fly through the air. Give it extra power by flicking the hand holding the spoon as you let it go. Make sure you don't splatter anyone!

Challenge someone else to a competition and mark your scores here:

Date completed: Day __27TH__ Month __June__ Year __2015__

16. MAKE DAMPER BREAD OVER A FIRE

This food is guaranteed to get everyone messy

What you need:

- 500g self-raising flour
- 300-500ml of water
- A mixing bowl
- A long wooden stick about as thick as your finger
- Fire pit (make sure the fire is fully extinguished after you've finished)
- An adult to help you

TOP TIP

Mix butter, brown sugar and cinnamon together, spread it on the top of your cooked damper bread and put it back over the fire to melt.

Put the flour in the bowl and slowly add the water. Mix the dough with your hands, adding a little flour if it gets too sticky. After a while the sticky dough will become firmer, but this will take lots of arm power. Once your dough is ready take a handful and roll it into a sausage. Wind the sausage around the top part of the stick so that it looks like a helter-skelter slide, then carefully hold the stick on one end so that the dough is over the fire, making sure that you keep your hands well away from the side of the fire pit. Your damper bread will take about 15-20 minutes to cook and you will need to keep turning it so that each side cooks evenly. Once the sides start to go brown it's ready to eat, but watch out, it will be very hot.

Try out some different fillings for your damper bread. Which is your favourite?

Damper bread is a traditional Australian bread which was made by early settlers when they set off to explore this unknown land.

Date completed: Day _____ Month _____ Year _____

17. CREATE A MASTERPIECE WITH NATURAL PAINTS

What colours will you make?

What you need:

- Empty jars with lids
- A stone for grinding or a stick for stirring
- Wild ingredients
- A brush
- Egg yolk
- A piece of wood or anything you like to paint on!

TOP TIP

You can also use things around your home to make paints. Spices, ground-up clay plant pots and beetroot all make amazing colours (but get permission to use them first!).

Blackberries, mud or charcoal all make fantastic paints. Grind them in pots with a stone or a stick to release the juices and colour. Adding an egg will help your paint stick together and make it glossy. Now you can then use your brush or your hands to create your masterpiece.

Paint examples of the colours you made here:

I used blue

I used Purple

I used green

I used pink

I used red

I used yellow

Go on a guided fungi walk and ask the leader to show you ink caps, a mushroom used in the past to make ink.

Date completed: Day _25^TH_ Month _November_ Year _2016_

18. THROW SEED BOMBS

Wild flowers are beautiful and great for wildlife

What you need:

- Native wild flower seeds
- Peat-free compost
- Clay powder
- Mixing bowl
- Spoon
- Water in a bottle or watering can

> **TOP TIP**
>
> Add water a drip at a time so your clay does not become too sloppy. It needs to be like play dough so you can roll it into egg-sized balls.

Mix together a pinch of compost and a pinch of wild flower seeds with a handful of clay powder in a bowl. Slowly add water and mix it all up with your hands. Roll into balls and dry them in the sunshine to for about a day. Now head out and start flower bombing by throwing them wherever you think wild flowers might love to grow. Slowly the sun and rain will break down the bomb and the seeds will start to grow.

Have a look at the wild flowers growing near your house; draw your favourite one here.

Date completed: Day _8TH_ Month _December_ Year _2016_

19. DREAM UP A MINIATURE WORLD

Get on your hands and knees for this tiny adventure

What you need:

- ✓ – Natural materials
- ✓ – String, card and scissors are all optional

Create your miniature world by looking for natural materials which might make good doorways, windows and pathways. Find a hole in a tree or a nook under a root and set up a doorway, windows, flowerbeds, a tiny ladder; be as creative as you can. You can use string or twigs to make bridges between trees and start building a whole town!

TOP TIP

If you find a pine tree you might find sticky sap oozing out of the bark. Make a string ladder and stick it to the tree using the sap then make a new doorway out of mud and sticks at the top to create the ultimate top floor flat.

Take a photo of your miniature creation and stick it here:

Date completed: Day _29TH_ Month _October_ Year _2016_

20. CARVE A PUMPKIN LANTERN

Who can make the scariest face?

What you need:

- One pumpkin, the bigger the better
- A sharp knife
- A small tea light candle
- A bowl for the insides
- A grown-up to help you

TOP TIP

Save the pumpkin seeds and bake them in the oven for a yummy snack!

Cut the top off your pumpkin with the help of a grown-up then roll up your sleeves and scoop out the gloopy, sticky centre with your hands or a spoon. You can then use the knife to cut out pieces to make a face or a pattern. Make sure you are really careful when cutting them out.

Once night has fallen, add your candle and draw a picture of your glowing lantern on this page.

In Somerset the Thursday before Hallowe'en is called Punky Night. Traditionally children carve pumpkins and go from house to house asking for a candle.

Date completed: Day 30TH Month October Year 2016

MUCKY

 21. Leave monster tracks ✓

 22. Become a worm charmer

 23. Build a conker run ✓

 24. Help out on a farm ✓

 25. Brew a stinky magic potion

 26. Dry your own mud bricks

 27. Make feely boxes

 28. Dissect an owl pellet

 29. Set up a mud kitchen

 30. Grow seedy socks

21. LEAVE MONSTER TRACKS

Create your own legend

What you need:
- Sticks
- Your hands
- Mud

Huge footprints left in the mud and the snow have made some people believe there are monsters, such as Big Foot and the Yeti. Make your own monster footprints by finding a good patch of mud and using sticks and your hands to mark out an enormous foot shape. You could create a giant human foot, a paw or something even more mysterious.

What shape was your monster's foot? Draw it here.

Date completed: Day 23RD   Month August   Year 2016

22. BECOME A WORM CHARMER

Bang, stamp and shout, see those worms come crawling out!

What you need:

- Pots, pans, trumpets – anything which makes a noise
- A garden fork
- A stick
- A patch of earth
- Water

TOP TIP

Make sure you look after your worms by making them a comfortable place to wait before the big count. Put some damp soil in a jar and place the worms carefully inside. Make sure to keep it out of the sun and return them to the ground as soon as possible.

You charm worms by making the soil vibrate. The worm will think it's a hungry mole and head to the surface to escape. You can do this by putting a garden fork in the earth and hitting the handle to make the metal part vibrate under the soil. You can also bang pots and pans or play your musical instrument near to the earth, the louder the better! Carefully turn the top layer of soil over in your hands to see if the worms are starting to appear.

How many worms did you charm today?

The first worm charming world record was set in 1980 by Mr Tom Shufflebotham who raised 511 worms in half an hour.

Date completed: Day _____ Month _____ Year _____

23. BUILD A CONKER RUN

How far can your conker roll along
your home-made run?

What you need:

- A collection of conkers or other
  large seeds such as acorns
- Natural construction material

Find some conkers and see what
you can use around you to make
a run. Start by propping one end
of a piece of bark up so that your
conker rolls downhill and then
see what else you can use to
keep it rolling. Perhaps take some materials
from home with you, such as cardboard tubes. Remember to take them
home again when you are finished.

Which was your most ingenious part of your conker run design? Sketch it
here so you remember it for next time.

I got lost and I put conkers where I had been.

The World
Conker Championships
are held every year
on the second
Sunday in October in
Northamptonshire.

Date completed: Day __28TH__ Month __September__ Year __2015__

24. HELP OUT ON A FARM

Muck out a stable or sweep the yard, there is always lots to do!

What you need:

– Access to a farm

– Wellies

– An adult to help

Farmers have to work very hard and it is often a very messy business. Ask a grown-up to help you find a farmer who would like some help and see what jobs you can do. Things like cleaning out a slimy water tank, sweeping a yard or mixing grain with your hands will give you a great chance to see what goes on in a real farmyard.

Make sure that you keep clear of farm machinery and take care to thoroughly wash your hands at the end of the activity.

What did you do at the farm today?: I fed the sheep. I gave the horses polos. I used the sheep dog to round up the sheep.

Date completed: Day **17TH** Month **June** Year **2010**

25. BREW A STINKY MAGIC POTION

Try making several different ones

What you need:

- A jar or pot with a lid
- A stick for mixing
- Water
- Potion ingredients

TOP TIP

When you have finished your potion, try adding bicarbonate of soda and vinegar to the jar and watch it bubble up.

Take your bottle and fill it with wild ingredients that you find whilst exploring outdoors. Use a stick to mush it all up then add some water. Put the cap on and shake it hard. Your potion can include anything you want. Blackberries or soil will give it colour, whilst mud will make it thicker. The kind of magic potion it is might inspire what you put in it. If it is a potion which turns you into a fish, you might need sea water and scale-shaped leaves. If it's meant to make you really small you might look for tiny pieces. Don't drink it though; this is a potion for the nostrils only!

Imagine what your magic potion might do and write it here:

Date completed: Day _____ Month _____ Year _____

26. DRY YOUR OWN MUD BRICKS

What will you build?

What you need:

- Mud
- Ice cube tray
- Soil

TOP TIP

Mix glitter into your mud to create bricks which will shine in the sun.

For bricks you need your mud to feel like biscuit dough. If it's too runny add soil; if it is too thick add some water. Squish your mud into ice cube trays and leave in the sun until they dry out. You should then be able to tap them out. Build a miniature wall using wet mud to stick the bricks together.

What did you build with your bricks?

Date completed: Day _____ Month _____ Year _____

27. MAKE FEELY BOXES
No peeking!

What you need:

- Boxes
- Natural treasures to go inside

Challenge your friends and family
to reach into a box with their eyes
closed and guess what is inside.
Fill each box with a different
natural thing. Take time to feel it with your
eyes closed to imagine what it might be like for them. You can make some
things even stranger. Try cutting acorns and conkers in half, for example,
which will give them one slightly slimy side. That's sure to confuse the person
reaching in.

Draw your friends and family's faces when they put their hands in!

TOP TIP

Give each box a messy rating and
see how many of your friends and
family dare put their hands in.

Date completed: Day __16ᵀᴴ__ Month __November__ Year __2012__

28. DISSECT AN OWL PELLET

Become a real nature detective

What you need:

- An owl pellet
- Water
- Small bowl
- Shallow dish/tray
- Tweezers/Cocktail sticks
- Disinfectant
- Magnifying glass
- Newspaper
- Surgical gloves (like the ones found in a first aid kit)

TOP TIP

Place each thing you find on a clean sheet of newspaper. You will be able to see what the owl ate recently. Things to watch out for include skulls, jaw bones with tiny teeth, beetle wings and fur.

Birds like kestrels, sparrowhawks and owls eat their prey whole but they only digest the parts which are nutritious. They cough up the other parts such as bones, teeth and fur in sausage-shaped objects called pellets. By looking at the pellets you can work out what the bird has been eating. Pellets are easier to pull apart when they have been soaked, so put some water in your bowl, add a few drops of disinfectant, and put your pellet in for about half an hour. Remove your pellet from the water and blot it dry with newspaper. Use the tweezers or cocktail sticks to tease your pellet apart.

Stick your favourite bones to this page using strong glue.

Date completed: Day _____ Month _____ Year _____

29. SET UP A MUD KITCHEN

Mud pancake anyone?

What you need:

- Mud
- Pots and pans
- Water
- Spoons
- Jars and squeezy bottles
- Any other kitchen tools you can convince your parents to let go of!

TOP TIP

Add petals, leaves and grass to your mud recipes to give your muddy meals a colour boost.

Set up your mud kitchen in your garden. Think about your favourite meal and see if you can make a muddy version. Fill squeezy bottles with runny mud to act as ketchup and try making tiny mud peas. The ultimate challenge though will be to flip a mud pancake!

Write down your favourite mud recipe here:

Date completed: Day _____ Month _____ Year _____

30. GROW SEEDY SOCKS

What grew in your seedy socks?

What you need:

- A pair of socks
- Soil
- A pot

Some seeds have tiny hooks that attach them to the fur of passing animals or to your clothes. This helps them to travel to new places where they can grow. Wear an old pair of socks over your shoes and run around in a wild flower meadow. Then take them off and carefully turn them inside out before stuffing them with soil and planting them in a pot. Water it and wait!

The largest seeds in the world come from a type of palm tree called a coco de mer.

Date completed: Day _____ Month _____ Year _____

CROCODILE

GRUBBY

31. Give a tree a face ✓

32. Make an earth angel ✓

33. Disappear into the landscape ✓

34. Make a charcoal pencil

35. Build a sand sea monster ✓

36. Create a wild assault course

37. Make patterns with sand ✓

38. Build a wormery

39. Make chalk prints ✓

40. Build a scarecrow ✓

31. GIVE A TREE A FACE

What's the story behind your tree?

What you need:

- A tree
- Some clay
- Sticks, moss and anything else you find

TOP TIP

Look for face-like features on a tree trunk to start you off. A knot in the wood could make an excellent bumpy nose or you might spot some moss growing in the shape of bushy eyebrows.

First find your tree. Ones with rough bark are easiest to stick clay to. Use the clay to start building a face onto the trunk. Try to sculpt a big nose and some lips. Use a little bit of water with the clay to help mush it into the trunk and smooth the surface. Add natural materials to your face such as acorns for eyes or leaves for ears.

Write about the tree person you've created here. Give them a name – how old are they?:

~~Their~~ name is skoopy and he is 13 years old. I used string to tie in a big knot for the nose. I used bush for eyebrows.

Date completed: Day __23RD__ Month __Febuary__ Year __2014__

52

32. MAKE AN EARTH ANGEL

Sand, snow or dust, you can make angels anywhere

What you need:

– Yourself!

– A good patch of ground

– Sticks, blades of grass and anything else you find

Find a good patch of undisturbed earth for your angel. It will need to be covered in fresh snow, fallen leaves or loose dust or sand. Lie on your back and move your legs in and out and your arms up and down, making sure you keep them nice and straight like you're doing a star jump. When you think you've made a mark get up carefully and jump away from your angel. You can add other details if you've like. Give the wings detail with long blades of grass or make a halo of driftwood.

Try and make earth angels in as many places as you can. Keep a list of the places where you left angels here:

snow. With my At grance in the
dirt, flinger on the

Date completed: Day _27TH_ Month _December_ Year _2015_

33. DISAPPEAR INTO THE LANDSCAPE

Camouflage yourself and disappear

What you need:

- Natural objects
- Old clothes with lots of pockets
- String

Camouflage means blending in with the space around you. Take a look at the space that you are in. Are most things in that area a similar colour like greens or browns, or are there lots of trees, bushes or rocks? Your challenge is to look as similar as possible to the world around you, so using natural materials is a great start. Attach natural materials to yourself by peaking them out of your pockets, cuffs or your waistband or hold big pieces like chucks of bark or big clumps of leaves in place using string. You will probably need help with this challenge!

Challenge someone to a game of hide and seek.

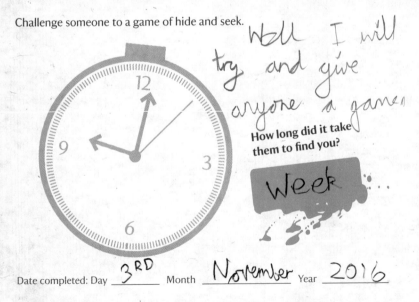

Well I will try and give anyone a game

How long did it take them to find you?

Week

Date completed: Day 3RD Month November Year 2016

34. MAKE A CHARCOAL PENCIL

Biscuit tins at the ready!

What you need:

- One empty metal tin, eg. an old biscuit, chocolates or coffee tin
- A fire pit (make sure that the fire is extinguished after you've finished)
- Wood (try to make all of it the same thickness and from the same tree)
- A pair of loppers (large scissors for cutting wood)
- A hammer

- A large nail
- Fireproof gloves
- An adult to help

Use your hammer and nail to punch five holes through your tin lid. Cut twigs to the same height as your tin and stack them in next to each other. Put the lid on your tin and place it all on the fire – make sure you are wearing your fireproof gloves. You will see steam and smoke come out of the holes, then gas, which will catch fire. Once all this has died down your charcoal is ready! This should take about an hour. Remove from the fire using the fireproof gloves and turn it upside down to cool so no air sneaks into your oven for 24 hours.

Use this page as your charcoal sketch pad.

Date completed: Day _____ Month _____ Year _____

35. BUILD A SAND SEA MONSTER

Surprise and scare people on the beach!

What you need:

- Sand
- Whatever you find on the beach

Monsters of the deep have always been spotted as their humps and tails appear out of the water. Find a patch of beach and build humps and a tail out of sand. At the end, create a terrifying head and decorate your beast with natural things found around you – try shells, pebbles or seaweed.

TOP TIP

Dig down around the humps, tail and head to create a moat around your beast. Then dig a channel from your moat to the sea and watch the water flood in and surround your sea monster.

What is your terrifying sea monster called? What does it like to eat?

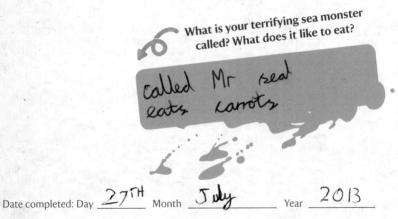

called Mr seal
eats carrots

Date completed: Day **27TH** Month **July** Year **2013**

36. CREATE A WILD ASSAULT COURSE

Jump, wriggle, crawl and slide through your own assault course

What you need:

- Inspiration from the world around you

Create your own assault course challenge. Weave in and out of trees, crawl under a fallen branch or balance along a fallen trunk. Make your challenges as creative as you can. Who's up for mud limbo, moss balancing or puddle jumping?

TOP TIP

A wild assault course on a beach can use sand to create humps to climb over as well as some tricky water jumps.

Draw a map of your assault course challenge here:

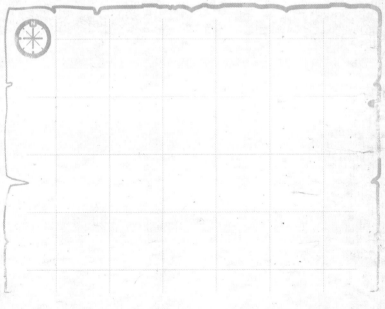

Date completed: Day _____ Month _____ Year _____

37. MAKE PATTERNS WITH SAND

String up a bag of sand, cut a hole in the bottom and off we go!

What you need:

- A plastic bag
- Sand
- A tree branch
- String

Collect sand in a bag and tie the top to a branch with string. Clear an area under the bag, then cut a very small hole in the bottom and start swinging the bag back and forth, side to side and round and round as the sand starts trickling out. Try writing your name with the sand or drawing a simple picture.

Recreate the pattern your made on the ground here using glue, then sprinkle sand on the page before shaking it all off and revealing the pattern:

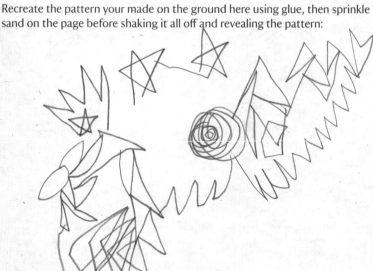

Date completed: Day _27TH_ Month _July_ Year _2013_

38. BUILD A WORMERY
These wiggly wonders make great compost for your garden

What you need:

- Worms
- A box made from glass, wood or plastic
- Compostable material
- Shredded newspaper
- Moss

TOP TIP

Add finely crushed egg shells to give your worms some extra calcium.

Fill your box with a mix of moss and shredded paper and make it moist but not dripping. Add your compostable material (see number 1 for tips on what is good to use). At the top finish with another layer of your newspaper and moss mix and add your worms. After three months your compost will be ready to spread on the garden. Keep your worms to do it all over again, or return them to the great outdoors to let them carry on their work under the ground.

Write the date you started your wormery here so you know when three months have passed:

28TH January 2015

I let them go on 28TH March 2015

Worms breathe through their skin

Do they

Wow

Date completed: Day _28TH_ Month _January_ Year _2015_

39. MAKE CHALK PRINTS

Get creative, naturally!

What you need:

- Chalk (If you can't find any natural chalk use blackboard chalk)
- Black paper (optional)

TOP TIP

If you find natural chalk you can also use it as a natural paint for number 17.

Chalk is actually a rock and can be found naturally all over east and south England. Look out for telltale bits of white rock. If you find some, use a harder rock to crush it into a powder before covering your hands in it and creating fantastic prints on black paper.

Do a chalk drawing here:

Date completed: Day __16TH__ Month __September__ Year __2015__

40. BUILD A SCARECROW
Will yours scare birds?

What you need:

- ✓ – A pillowcase
- ⌡ – An old shirt and trousers and accessories
- ⌡ – Two long sticks/ branch
- ✗ – String and sticky tape
- ⋏ – Permanent markers
- ⌡ – Lots of straw
- ✗ – Newspaper

> **TOP TIP**
>
> You can see some fantastically scary scarecrow examples at the Quarry Bank Mill summer scarecrow festival.

First, make the frame by tying the sticks in a cross shape. Dress your sticks with the clothes then push the bottom stick into the ground. Use the straw and scrunched up newspaper to fill the clothes and tie the trouser and shirt ends so all the stuffing does not fall out. Make a head by stuffing the pillowcase, drawing the face on and then add it to the top, tying it on tightly.

Take a photo of you with your scarecrow and stick it here:

> Scarecrows are known by different names all over Britain including tattybogles, shoy-hoys, jacks-of-straw and hodmedods.

Date completed: Day **14TH** Month **June** Year **2010**

SOGGY

41. Become a welly engineer

42. Paint with water

43. Go on a puddle hunt ✓

44. Give a toad a home

45. Have a water relay ✓

46. Go on a seaweed safari

47. Bridge a puddle

48. Make your own bubble wand

49. Go on a wet welly walk

50. Set out a snail picnic

41. BECOME A WELLY ENGINEER

Get friends and family involved to change the course of the water

What you need:

- Wellies

When it rains heavily water will pour down pathways. Get outside and get your wellies on. If you put your foot horizontal to a fast stream of water it will splash upwards and over your welly. If you put your foot to an angle however the water will flow off to the side. If you can get a group of people together you can make the water zigzag down the hill.

TOP TIP

See if you can divert the water to somewhere useful like a flowerbed or a pond.

How many people did you manage to get to help you?

Date completed: Day _____ Month _____ Year _____

42. PAINT WITH WATER

How long will your painting last?

What you need:

- Water
- A bottle

TOP TIP

When it snows, mix mud, spices or cooked beetroot in water before you sprinkle it on the snow to create a colourful masterpiece.

The best thing about painting with water is that you can do it on almost any outdoor surface. A patch of dust, sand or dry mud will work best. Fill a bottle with water and dribble it slowly onto the ground. Draw patterns and try and write your name before it fades. Can you create a masterpiece before it disappears or a water fight breaks out?

Practise your pattern here before trying it on the ground:

Date completed: Day __19TH__ Month __March__ Year __2015__

Which puddle has the best splash? The biggest

43. GO ON A PUDDLE HUNT

Who can find the biggest splash?

What you need:

– Wellies

On a rainy day, head out to find the best puddles. Do your biggest jump in each puddle you find. Which puddle has the best splash? Who is the splash champion? *it is me Of course*

Draw a splash-o-meter to measure which is the best puddle. What do you think makes a great puddle? *rain*

Yes I Do Think It Is Rain I like going splash in puddles,

Date completed: Day _17TH_ Month _April_ Year _2015_

44. GIVE A TOAD
A HOME
Create a toad paradise in your garden

What you need:

- A clay plant pot
- A trowel
- A shady spot, ideally near some water
- A patch of earth
- A grown-up to help you

> **TOP TIP**
>
> Your toad needs some privacy to feel at home. However you can track his comings and goings by watering the area around the entrance to the toad home until it turns to mud. You'll see his tracks as he comes in and out.

Toads love a damp and shady space to hide. Take an old clay plant pot and, with some adult help, knock a small section from the rim. Turn it upside down on the ground and the part you took out should look like a little cave entrance. Place it somewhere shaded and close to water and wait for someone to move in. Why not decorate your toad home with mud or natural paints? *With that idea I will*

Do you know what toadspawn looks like? Find out and draw some here:

Common toads can live up to 40 years

I did not know that. I is that true

Date completed: Day _13TH_ Month _February_ Year _2013_

45. HAVE A WATER RELAY

Get the water from the front of the line to the back as fast as you can!

What you need:

- A cup for each team member
- Two buckets
- Water
- Stopwatch

TOP TIP

Make this even messier by pouring the water from cup to cup whilst the cup is held over the head of the next person in line.

Gather together a group of friends or family for this soggy challenge. Two teams will need to stand in rows, each team member behind the other. At the beginning or each line place a bucket full of water and put an empty bucket at the back of the line. Finally, give each team member a cup. Both teams then have two minutes to pass as much water as possible from cup to cup along the line from the front bucket to the back one. The person passing the water is not allowed to look behind them at any time. Failure to work as a team will mean water everywhere but the bucket!

Who was the most wet at the end?

I was

Date completed: Day **5TH** Month **January** Year **2014**

46. GO ON A SEAWEED SAFARI

Slimy or soft, what kinds of seaweed will you find?

What you need:

- A rocky seashore
- Shoes that you don't mind getting wet

The rocky shore is an amazing place to go exploring. Watch your step as you explore the rock pools. Lift out some seaweed to get a close look. Feel it, smell it, flip it over and see if anything is stuck to it. Try to find slimy or red seaweed or some that is full of air sacks that help it to float.

TOP TIP

To give yourself the best chance of finding lots of types of seaweed go hunting at low tide and work your way up the beach as the tide comes in.

Dry your favourite piece of seaweed in the sun and then stick it to this page:

Seaweed feels rubbery because it needs a thick skin to protect it from sea salt.

Date completed: Day _____ Month _____ Year _____

69

47. BRIDGE A PUDDLE

Test your balance and your building skill

What you need:

- A puddle
- Wood and other natural materials

Find a long and wide puddle to cross. You have 15 minutes to build your bridge before you have to try it out. Use sticks, logs and stones to create a path across the puddle from one side to the other. If you're feeling extra confident take your wellies off and make your way across in your socks. Just hope you don't fall in!

All great bridges have wonderful descriptive names such a Tower Bridge, the Golden Gate Bridge and Iron Bridge.

Write what you called your bridge here:

> **TOP TIP**
>
> Stones and sticks can be very slippery, so try to keep the top of them dry as you are putting them in place.

Fixy Dixy Bridge

Date completed: Day 17TH Month April Year 2013

48. MAKE YOUR OWN BUBBLE WAND

How big can you make your bubbles?

What you need:

- Two sticks
- String
- 1 washer
- One mug full of washing-up liquid
- Half a mug full of cornflour mixed with a little water
- A bowl

TOP TIP

Make sure all string is dipped in the bubble mix. Lift the bubble wand out, keeping the top of the sticks as close together as possible. Open the wand up very slowly and start to walk backwards. Your bubble will start getting bigger and bigger. To set it free, just cross your sticks over each other and watch it go.

Measure a piece of string that stretches from one hand to another when you hold your arms out to the sides. Attach one end of the string to the top of one stick and then thread the washer onto the string before tying the other end to the top of the other stick. Attach another piece of string one arm's length long between the tops of the two sticks so you end up with a triangle of string. Mix the washing up liquid and cornflour in a bowl and you are ready to make some giant bubbles.

Draw a picture of you and your biggest bubble here:

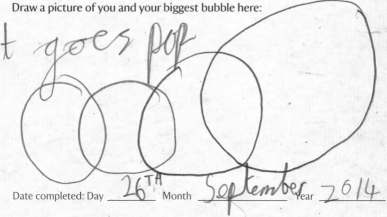

I t goes pop

Date completed: Day ___26TH___ Month ___September___ Year ___2014___

49. GO ON A WET WELLY WALK

Can you avoid wet socks?

What you need:

- You
- Your wellies
- The great outdoors

The fantastic thing about wellies is that you can confidently walk in all kinds of places. On this walk see how much you can jump in mud or a puddle before the mud goes over your wellies.

> **TOP TIP**
>
> If your wellies do get full up with water, why don't you have a wet welly throwing competition? Fill them with water and throw them as far as you can or keep them on, full of water and have a race.

Draw a line on this welly to show how far you dared to go:

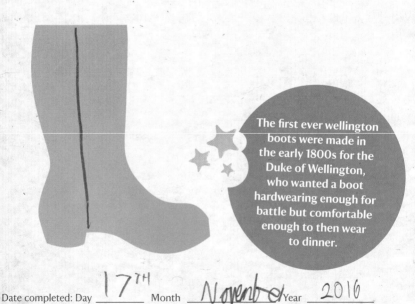

> The first ever wellington boots were made in the early 1800s for the Duke of Wellington, who wanted a boot hardwearing enough for battle but comfortable enough to then wear to dinner.

Date completed: Day _17TH_ Month _November_ Year _2016_

50. SET OUT A SNAIL PICNIC

What do you think might tempt a snail to tea?

What you need:

- Vegetable scraps
- Leaves and moss
- Plain paper

Snails love damp places. A perfect setting for a snail picnic would be a wet patch of ground with a few hiding places nearby.

Set out a square of paper as a picnic blanket which will double as a tasty snail snack. Leave a pile of carrot and cucumber scraps and another of greenery found nearby and wait for the snails to find it.

When the snails have finished their picnic take what is left of the picnic blanket and stick it here:

Snails cannot see very well but they have an excellent sense of smell.

When they get to your picnic they will be using around 14,000 teeth to munch through that lunch.

Date completed: Day _____ Month _____ Year _____

73

10 BEST MESSY THINGS TO DO

1

DID YOU KNOW?

You can add extra fun to your barefoot painting by placing different size and shape leaves on your paper before you step over them with your muddy feet. When you're done, carefully lift the leaves up and see their silhouettes!

8. BAREFOOT PAINTING

(page 23)

That is very strange

25. BREW A STINKY MAGIC POTION

(page 44)

DID YOU KNOW?

If you want to make your potion extra stinky, leave it in a warm place for a few days to let the smells brew. A warm, sunny window ledge or airing cupboard are perfect hideaways! Poo-ee. Nose pegs at the ready!

2

18. THROW SEED BOMBS

I have don 'it but 'it did not do that

(page 35)

your wrong

Dont read

DID YOU KNOW?

You can add a few chili flakes to your seed bomb mix to protect the seeds from turning into a tasty treat for ants, birds and slugs. Keep your hands away from your eyes and be sure to wash your hands afterwards.

15 TARGET PRACTICE WITH MUD AND A SPOON

(page 32)

DID YOU KNOW?

You can make the competition harder by throwing the mud at the target from further away. Try starting just a few steps away from the target, then move back a few more steps each time and see how you score.

4

21. LEAVE MONSTER TRACKS

5

(page 40)

DID YOU KNOW?

Why not try digging a bit deeper when you're making your monster tracks? The deeper the footprint, the heavier the mysterious creature that left it...

6

DID YOU KNOW?

Your eyes are one of the most likely things to get you spotted, so don't forget to close them when you're hiding!

33. DISAPPEAR INTO THE LANDSCAPE

(page 54)

38.
BUILD A
WORMERY

(page 59)

7

(page 59)

DID YOU KNOW?

Worms like a warm and moist home and work best when they are comfortable. Keep your wormery sheltered from bad weather and cold temperatures. You can always leave it inside a garden shed, but get a grown-up's permission.

Lets have fun with puddles

8

43. GO ON A PUDDLE HUNT
(page 66)

DID YOU KNOW?

Lots of different creatures like birds and small mammals drink puddle water. Some insects even use puddles as their homes, so have a closer look at the puddle before you splash in it to see if there's anything interesting living there!

Lets make a brack with bubbles

9

48. MAKE YOUR OWN BUBBLE WAND

(page 71)

9. HELP BUILD A COB WALL

(page 24)

10

DID YOU KNOW?

Cob is the perfect material for building a hiding place for frogs and other small creatures. Why not make a small cave shape and leave it underneath a bush or somewhere quiet and see who moves in...

Spring

1

14. BUILD A GIANT NEST

Spring is a busy time for birds building nests for their babies. Why not join in and see how long it takes you to make your nest? When you've made it, try sitting inside in different weather – is it warm and cosy? Does it give you shelter from the wind?

Nest

2

22. BECOME A WORM CHARMER

Bang, clatter, smash and shake those pans. You might need to warn your neighbours you're going to be worm charming otherwise they will wonder what you're doing! Why not invite some friends to join in and together you can make even more noise...

30. GROW SEEDY SOCKS

Can you count how many seeds are stuck to the socks before you fill it with soil? Make a note of it, then see how many seedlings grow. Will it be the same number?

40. BUILD A SCARECROW

Try making different kinds of scarecrow monsters, aliens and other weird and wonderful creatures – they'll be sure to scare those crows away!

37. MAKE PATTERNS WITH SAND

If you can't find a tree, try holding the bag yourself and slowly spinning around in a circle getting a little faster each time you go around. When the bag is empty (and you've stopped feeling dizzy!) you may be able to see a spiral shape just like a snail's shell. Try spinning at different speeds to make other size and shape spirals.

THE BEST THINGS TO DO IN

Summer

1

17. CREATE A MASTERPIECE WITH NATURAL PAINTS

This is a good one to do during the summer months because there are many wonderful colourful ingredients available outside. Once you've made your paint, dip pebbles and other bits like twigs and leaves into the mix and press them onto your canvas to make interesting patterns, shapes and textures.

2

26. DRY YOUR OWN MUD BRICKS

If you want to make larger mud bricks, collect empty butter or ice cream cartons and fill them with the muddy mixture and leave out in the sun to dry (they will take a bit longer because they are bigger).

31. GIVE A TREE A FACE

This is a great one to do at different times of the year, but especially in the summer because trees have all their leaves on, which look like their hair!

3

35. BUILD A SAND SEA MONSTER

Use a stick as a pencil and write the terrifying name of your monster in the sand around it – in the largest letters you can imagine. People will see it from far away!

4

5

50. SET OUT A SNAIL PICNIC

Look out for signs of silvery snail trails to see how many have visited your picnic.

THE BEST THINGS TO DO IN

Autumn

20. CARVE A PUMPKIN LANTERN

Using a black marker or similar, draw your face or pattern onto the pumpkin first before you start cutting it out – this will help you get the shape right. Other good ideas for pumpkin carvings are: a squirrel shape (nice big curves that are easy enough to cut around), a heart shape, a letter of the alphabet. Stars work nicely, too.

1

2

23. BUILD A CONKER RUN

Race your friends and see if the size of the conker makes a difference to the speed it rolls down the ramps you have built.

2. SLIP DOWN A MUD SLIDE

Forwards, backwards, feet first, head first! See which way makes you go the fastest!

12. MAKE TOFFEE APPLES

Toffee apples can make wonderful gifts – all you need to do is attach a ribbon or bow to the lolly stick and put the whole thing into a nice gift bag.

29. SET UP A MUD KITCHEN

Who needs real food when you've got mud food? Scoop it, roll it, dollop it – but don't really eat it!

THE BEST THINGS TO DO IN

Winter

1

3. MAKE A FAT BALL BIRD FEEDER

Make five or more fat balls and keep them stored away ready to bring out when the last one has been eaten. The birds and other wildlife will appreciate a steady supply of food through the winter months right through into the spring.

2

41. BECOME A WELLY ENGINEER

When the weather gets wet, it's time to get your wellies on and start adventuring outside. The wetter the better!

47. BRIDGE A PUDDLE

When you've crossed the puddle, put your wellies back on and see if you can jump across the puddle in one go – but be ready for a big splash if you don't quite make it!

49. GO ON A WET WELLY WALK

You can use your boots to measure how deep each puddle is. Before you set off on your wet welly walk, use stickers or tape to mark measurements onto your wellies (ideally in centimetres). Each time you go into a puddle, you'll be able to see where the water comes up to and therefore know how deep the puddle is!

Write down the different depths of your puddle here

39. MAKE CHALK PRINTS

If the weather is too bad to play out, you can bring this little project inside. If you want to experiment with texture, put objects (like pieces of bark, rocks, feathers) underneath your black paper and rub the chalk over the top – you'll be amazed at the patterns that come through.

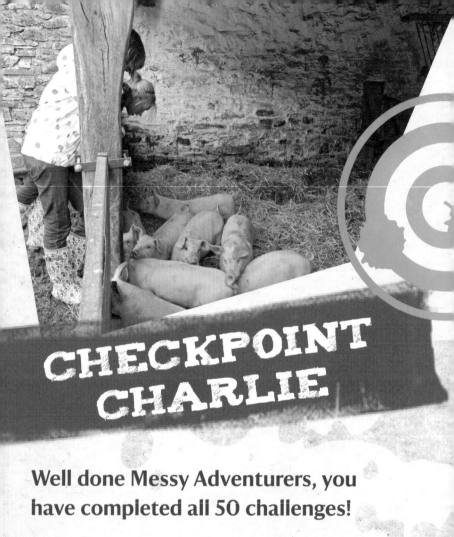

CHECKPOINT CHARLIE

Well done Messy Adventurers, you have completed all 50 challenges!

Write down which one was the:

MOST MESSY?

MOST FILTHY?

MOST GRUBBY?

MOST SOGGY?

MOST STICKY?

Alice

Alice

59 priory road
Kew, Richmond, Surrey
TW9 3JQ

Kilpatrick
Year 3

monday - school, ming
Tuesday - school, nothing
Wednesday - school, netball
Thursday - school, piano, brownies
Friday - school, nothing
Saturday - Ballet, Tap, Modern, flute, swimming
Sunday - church, nothing

It will
all change